SOMETHING F
TO THINK ABOUT

52 Modern-Day Parables
BY JIM COLLINS

Published in 2022 by Verité CM for Jim Collins

ISBN: 978-1-914388-25-5

Cover design, typesetting and production management by
Verité CM Ltd, Worthing, West Sussex UK +44 (0) 1903 241975

Printed in England

Contents

Foreword

Having been in Christian retail bookselling for over 30 years I am very aware of the power of the written word of God and how a book can change a person's life or have a very positive effect on how they think and relate to the broken world in which we live.

I like the title of this book because the author is asking us to think about what we are reading, assimilate and relate it to ourselves.

The Bible says we are 'Fearfully and wonderfully made' – (Psalm 139: verse 14.). The human brain is superior to any other created species. The brain has many functions but among them is our ability for perception, thinking, reasoning and memory.

It is possible to read the Bible like a history book and fail to relate and implement the word of God into our everyday lives.

Jesus was a great 'storyteller' during his Ministry on Earth which is demonstrated in the parables that he told.

Jim Collins – in this book of 52 Modern-Day Parables – continues a theme of his three previous books – asking us to think and relate events in our lives to our faith.

Jim has a gift of relating everyday events in his life to the Word of God which is both interesting and meaningful.

This book could really change your life if you take the time to think deeply about what is being said and ask yourself the question – 'What does this mean to me and how should I respond?"

I pray you will enjoy and be challenged by this book.

Roy Brittle
Choice Words Christian Bookshops

"... a book can change a person's life or have a very positive effect on how they think and relate to the broken world in which we live."

Introduction

Welcome to my latest book publication 'Something Further To Think About' bringing you a further selection of modern-day parables, to help you see and consider what God has to say about everyday experiences and events that we either encounter personally or hear about on the news.

It's just a small book, but it points to the best book that anyone could choose to read – the Bible.

Written by men, but inspired by the Spirit of God, the Bible gives direction, purpose and hope and reveals the way that we can know God personally through His Son Jesus Christ.

I hope in reading this further collection of 'devotional thoughts' you will be encouraged to read the Bible more and discover the 'bigger picture' for your life as God reveals His unique plan and purposes that He has for you.

Take time to think further on the scriptures you read. God promises to watch over His Word to fulfil it in our lives. May you know God's blessing and presence.

Jim Collins

*To George,
My precious prayer partner,
friend and encourager*

Happy New Year

At midnight on the 31st December, another year will close and a new one will commence. It will be the time when we say "Happy New Year" to those around us – or we may send texts and make phone calls to pass on our greetings to family and friends that live away.

The word happy has many meanings – but when we say to someone "Happy New Year" we are hoping they will have a pleasurable, cheerful and contented year.

In the bible – the Greek word used for happy is "blessed" – which is rich in meaning. To be blessed; includes a happiness produced by the experience of God's favour and salvation, regardless of our outward condition. It's a life-joy satisfaction that is found in God's grace shown towards us.

When Jesus taught the Beatitudes in His Sermon on the Mount, He revealed the "attitudes" we should have in our lives – that will result in us being blessed, happy and joyful.

Jesus said the poor and humble in spirit will be blessed – the meek, patient and long suffering will be blessed – the merciful will be blessed and receive mercy – and the pure in heart will be blessed for they shall see God – and the maintainers and makers of peace will be blessed. (Read Matthew 5:1-12)

The happiness and joy that God gives is not based on what we have or if things are going well – but in knowing God himself.

The well-known minister Charles Spurgeon said "It is not how much we have, but how much we enjoy, that makes happiness." We are to appreciate and be content with what we do have.

Concerning happiness being found in God – King David the psalmist declared "... in your presence there is fullness of joy; at your right hand are pleasures for evermore." (Psalm 16:11)

Jeremiah the prophet said "Blessed is the man who trusts in the Lord, whose trust "is" the Lord." (Jeremiah 17:7)

As we start a New Year – whatever we've been through or whatever lies before us – as we obey the Lord's commands and trust in His promises, we will discover true happiness.

We are blessed when we trust in the Lord

Gone fishing

When I was a boy, I loved going fishing. I spent many happy hours on the banks of the River Thames near Reading improving my angling skills. I enjoyed reading books about the subject and was willing to learn from other fishermen.

I recall on one of our family picnic fishing trips – I was being observed by a mature angler as I fished. Looking at the thickness of my line cast out across the water, he commented – "You could moor a boat with that!"

I never caught any good-size fish – although like most anglers, I do remember one big one that got away after breaking my line. If I caught just one fish, I would go home happy.

A few years ago, I captured the joy of Course fishing again when my wife and I had opportunity to go and do some fishing at a local lake. In just under 2 hours, we caught 26 fish between us.

In the Bible, Luke speaks of a boat fishing trip, which had not produced any catch. Jesus got into Simon's boat and when it was a little way from shore – He began to teach the crowds who had come to listen to him. When He had finished speaking; Jesus said to Simon, "Put out into the deep water, and let down the nets for a catch."

Simon answered, "Master, we've worked hard all night and haven't caught anything. But because you say so, I will let down the nets." (Luke 5:1-5)

Simon was a fisherman. He would have known his trade and methods. He could have thought, "This has just been a bad night, there's no fish around, and we'll try again tomorrow." However; Simon chose to heed the words of his Master Jesus.

When they obeyed and let down their nets – they caught such a large number of fish that their nets began to break. So they signalled to their partners in another boat to come and help them, and they came and filled both boats so full – that they began to sink. (Luke 5:6-7)

One of several things this story teaches us – is that Jesus is calling us to obey Him and to do things in the way that He asks. We can so easily set about our tasks in our own strength and ability.

This week, as we face situations that may appear fruitless and unproductive – remember that Jesus knows best; and will accomplish what is best for you as you trust in His Word and act on what He says.

When you obey
- without delay
then a miracle, a
mighty work can
start

Right direction

When I was taking a walk one day, a man stopped in his car and asked for directions to a road he was looking for. I thought hard, but had to apologise because I couldn't help him with the way to go.

A few days later; another person in a car stopped me as I was heading for home, and asked if I knew where a certain road was. This time, I did! Even better; he was so near; I was able to point to the road name sign which was only a short distance away. It is always good to be able to point someone in the right direction.

Being unable to find a road we are looking for; is not too drastic, compared to those times in our personal lives when we feel we have lost direction because of bad choices and decisions we may have made.

God knew that we would need help beyond ourselves when it came to going in the right direction for life; so He sent His Son Jesus to the world – and He says to each one of us "Follow me." God's way – is about walking in the foot-steps of Jesus.

As we choose to follow Jesus and obey His teaching, we will live out our lives – going in the right direction and experience the forgiveness and freedom He offers.

Jesus said "I am the way, and the truth and the life ..." (John 14:6) As we look to the Lord – He will guide us in the paths of righteousness for His name's sake." (Psalm 23:3)

To discover God's direction for our lives we will also need to acknowledge that His ways and His will is best.

Isaiah proclaimed God's word saying "For my thoughts are not your thoughts, neither are your ways my ways," declares the Lord. "As the heavens are higher than the earth, so are my ways higher than your ways and my thoughts than your thoughts." (Isaiah 55:8 9)

If you are in need of some direction right now – the Bible has a promise for you. "This God – His way is perfect; the word of the Lord proves true; He is a shield for all those who take refuge in Him." (Psalm 18:30 –ESV Bible)

God hears our prayers

Walking down our main street in the town, I heard a lady talking to someone on her mobile phone. She asked, "Did you get my text?" There can be many occasions when it is reassuring to know that someone has got a message we have sent.

If I am sending an urgent email, I will request a return receipt so I know it has been received. In addition, when I need to send important documents in the post, I use the "sign on receipt" – so I have the assurance that it has arrived safely.

There are many times when technology may fail us, and we are unable to send or receive messages to others. Throughout the pages of the Bible, you can read about the greatest means of communication that anyone can use – the gift of prayer, where we can talk to God – and be certain that He will hear and listen to every word that we speak to Him! (He even knows each word on our tongue before we speak them – Psalm 139:4)

Prayer is so much more than asking God to do things for us. Through prayer, we come to God through Jesus His Son – and we can share with Him all the things on our heart and mind.

As we share with God in prayer – we grow in our relationship with Him, and experience His love, care and guidance.

Sometimes, our prayers will not be answered in the way or the timing that we are hoping for.

One thing I have personally experienced about prayer is: "God always wants to do something in our lives when we pray to Him."

His delays to answering prayers are not denials.

As I await answers to prayer and read God's Word – He continues to teach me about: aspects of trust, priorities, right motives, attitudes in my life that need changing, and most of all: my need to acknowledge that He is Sovereign. God is in control – and in all things He works for the good of those who love Him. (Romans 8:28)

In your praying this week, remember that God has heard your request, and knows how best to answer what you are asking for – in His perfect timing.

Through prayer –
we grow in
our personal
relationship with
God

Believing for the best

I saw a cartoon recently which showed two people having a conversation about "not making assumptions." One commented – "You know what happens when you assume." The reply came – "I don't. Yet you are confidently asserting that I do."

Some years ago, I came out of a Betting shop with a handful of coins. Anyone observing, might have assumed that I'd won on a horse race. I'm not a gambling person – the money in my hand was payment for some vacuum cleaner bags that I had just delivered to a staff member in the shop.

Some years ago when I was on my way home from work – I may have been seen carrying a large, empty, cider bottle. From that; people could assume about my drinking habits – when all I had done was pick it up when I found it on the kerb-side. I was taking it home to re-cycle safely, to avoid it possibly becoming broken glass in the road.

It can be easy to make assumptions about people or situations, where we suppose something to be true or certain – without proof.

In the well-known scriptures of 1 Corinthians 13 – concerning love, the apostle Paul writes "... love bears all things, believes all things, hopes all things ..." (1 Corinthians 13:7 – New King James Version)

The love that we should have towards one another; is a love that looks for the opportunity to "believe the best" in – and for each other.

God demonstrated His own love towards us, in that while we were still sinners, Christ died for us." (Romans 5:8)

God didn't wait for us to "get our lives together – and in order" – before He came to us. He comes to us in our sinfulness and brokenness – to save, forgive and restore us when we call on His name. He believes in us – and wants us to experience His love, salvation and healing.

This week, we may meet someone who is longing for us to believe the best in them. Someone who needs another chance, is in need of our forgiveness or looking for encouragement to help them feel valued.

God says to us "Do nothing out of selfish ambition or vain conceit, but in humility consider others better than yourselves." (Philippians 2:3)

Love – believes
and looks for
the best in
one another

The real thing

When I was young (in the 70's) I had a Board game called "Masterpiece." This was an Art Auction game – where players bid against each other to purchase paintings by famous artists.

Each painting had a value card clipped to it (unknown to the bidder) – so it was possible to spend hundreds of thousands of pounds on a piece of art that may be valued at 1 million pounds; or at the worst, it could turn out to be a forgery.

I recall hearing about a painting bought for £400, which featured on the BBC's Antique Roadshow – had been revealed to be a Sir Anthony Van Dyck portrait by the 17th century Flemish Artist and was valued at £400, ooo.

The owner benefited from having an authentic masterpiece – and by selling it, was able to purchase some new bells for his Church. Many of us, may also have discovered that we own something that is genuine – and "it is valuable because it is the real thing."

This reminded me that the faith and trust, God wants us to have in Him – must also be genuine. The apostle Peter shared – "... though now for a little while you may have had to suffer grief in all kinds of trials. These have come so that your faith – of greater worth than gold ... may be proved genuine and may result in praise, glory and honour when Jesus Christ is revealed." (1 Peter 1:6-7)

Genuine faith sees trials and difficulties as opportunities to fully rely on God, instead of trying to do things in our own strength – and our way.

From my own experience, I have discovered that although going through trials is tough – they have been the times when I've learnt the most about trusting Jesus – setting new priorities and learning to see things from God's perspective. We are told to "Trust in the Lord with all your heart and lean not on your own understanding ..." (Proverbs 3:5)

If you're going through a testing time right now – remember that "genuine faith is like a muscle – it will grow stronger as it is exercised."

I encourage you to put your faith in God and the promises of His word. He says "... call upon Me in the day of trouble; I will deliver you, and you will honour me." (Psalm 50:15)

Faith in God –
turns difficulties
into opportunities

Love's greatest story

On Valentine's Day couples express their love and devotion for each other, with words, cards, chocolates, romantic dates – and for some it may involve a marriage proposal!

Many couples will watch a romantic movie on Valentine's Day. I have to confess that I like a good love story; and would prefer to see a happy ending, rather than a film that finishes leaving you unsure if the couple will "keep their love alive."

I was reading some feedback concerning what people look for in a good romantic movie. For some, they realise the couple may not be happy every day, but ultimately want them to live happily ever after.

Others see; falling and remaining in love as life's great adventure – and like any adventure this will involve challenges and uncertainty. It has also been commented that there has to be "something to keep the couple apart" (like distance or conflict) and where against the odds, things come together in the end. Even tragedy and crisis can deepen and strengthen love.

Throughout the pages of the Bible, we can read the words and see the unfolding of "Love's greatest story." In the book of Romans, we read that "God demonstrates His own love for us in this: While we were still sinners, Christ died for us." (Romans 5:8) Our sinfulness and selfishness are what keeps us "apart" from God.

In God's plan – for the world's greatest love story – He announces, "This is love: not that we loved God, but that

He loved us and sent His Son as an atoning sacrifice for our sins." (1 John 4:10) When we trust and seek after God, we will experience the greatness of His love towards us – which is steadfast and faithful. David the psalmist knew God's love for him when he declared – "How priceless is your unfailing love!" (Psalm 36:7)

As portrayed in some romantic films, we will all go through some dark days of doubt and seasons of sorrow. We will experience times when our hopes are shattered and our dreams fade. However: God's love endures through all things. The apostle Paul said, "I am convinced that neither death nor life ... neither the present nor the future ... nor anything else in all creation, will be able to separate us from the love of God that is in Christ Jesus our Lord." (Read Romans 8:37-39)

On Valentine's Day – remember that GOD IS LOVE, and as John wrote "... love one another, for love comes from God." (1 John 4:7)

Just looking

My wife and I went for a day trip to Exeter to have a look around the shops. I was browsing around one store, when I noticed a wooden post rack. I decided to purchase it – not to put letters in – but to use as a book stand, and the size and design of it was ideal for this purpose.

When I went to pay for it, the man behind the till asked me "Did you find what you were looking for today?"

The salesperson's question made me think further about this aspect of "seeking and finding."

Being human; we long to find love, security, significance, purpose, a sense of belonging and opportunities to contribute. In addition to these emotional needs – we will all have other things that we hope to find.

The Bible has much to say in guiding us about what we should be looking for in life. Jesus promised His disciples that if they sought first (above all else) God's kingdom and His righteousness, all the things that we need – would be given to us. (Read Matthew 6:25-34)

Seeking God's kingdom is to acknowledge that "God rules" in our lives – and over the world – and we do what He asks of us.

King David wrote ..." those who seek the Lord lack no good thing." (Psalm 34:10)

God's purpose for everyone is that we would seek Him – reach out for Him and find Him, though He is not far from each of us. For in Him we live and move and have our being. (Acts 17:27-28)

Jesus stands at the doorway of our lives and says "Ask and it will be given to you; seek and you will find; knock and the door will be opened to you. For everyone who asks receives; he who seeks finds; and to him who knocks, the door will be opened." (Matthew 7:7-8)

Have you found what you are looking for today?

In Jesus Christ you will find a friend and a Saviour; God himself, who will walk with you and never leave or forsake you. As you trust and obey His word – you will find that God is: faithful to His promises, rich in mercy, compassionate and gracious, slow to anger – and abounding in love.

In Jesus – you will find a Friend and a Saviour

Diesel spill

I was walking up from the town during a very heavy rain shower. As I looked at the channels of water – which were running rapidly down the hill – I noticed a rainbow-coloured sheen that indicated diesel had been spilt on the road surface.

It soon became apparent, the spill was over a large stretch of road and continued way beyond our house.

I am aware of the dangers of spilt diesel on roads – especially for those riding on two wheels.

When I got home, I immediately contacted the Council and informed them of the spillage. Within the hour; absorbent granules had been spread over the road – reducing the risk of people slipping and cars and bikes skidding.

Diesel spreads quickly in water and as it is oil – it does not evaporate. Spilt diesel can make a road as slippery as black ice.

This incident reminded me, that we will all experience circumstances in our lives when it seems like our feet are taken from under us. Our security and confidence are shaken. Things can be going well – and then suddenly there is a "slip up." Our plans and schedules don't work out as we hoped.

It is during these difficult situations that we can look to God for His help – and His solution.

In Psalm 94 – the writer proclaims of the Lord, "When I said, "My foot is slipping," your love O Lord supported me.

When anxiety was great within me, your consolation brought joy to my soul." (Psalm 94:18-19)

Sometimes we slip up – through making wrong decisions and doing things our way – instead of obeying what God says in His Word.

When we ask Jesus to forgive us – and seek to turn our lives around to follow Him – He will forgive us totally! He then lifts us up again so we can move on.

Jude wrote in praise of God's keeping power – "To Him who is able to keep you from falling and to present you before His glorious presence without fault and with great joy – to the only God our Saviour be glory ... through Jesus Christ our Lord" ... (Jude 24)

As you walk "your road of life" this week – be encouraged by the words of Habakkuk the prophet who said "The Sovereign Lord gives me strength. He makes me sure – footed as a deer and keeps me safe on the mountains." (Habakkuk 3:19 Good News Bible)

God is always ready to pick us up when we slip down

Word blocks

During a time out shopping, I was looking around a Home-ware gift shop and came across a selection of word blocks.

These decorative, wooden plaques spell out words like "Family, Love, Friends, Home, Relax ..." Some of the words of these ornaments will remind us of the things in life that are important to us or others.

I observed one that spelt "Believe" – and then another that read "Believe more!" On their own, these words pose a very open question for consideration. "Who or what are we to believe in – or believe more in?"

The Bible, from cover to cover – is God's word to us to enable us to "believe in Him" – to help us understand that He is the One who created us for a purpose – His purpose.

God's main plan for everyone is that we should know His Son Jesus as our Saviour, the One who saves us from our sins.

The disciples asked Jesus, "What must we do to do the works of God?" Jesus answered, "The work of God is this: to believe in the One He has sent." (John 6:28-29)

A father who brought his son to Jesus to be healed said "I do believe; but help me overcome my unbelief." (Mark 9:24) Like Thomas, we can all go through "days of doubt." (Read John 20:26-29)

I have discovered in my life, that when the difficult seasons come along; when I continue to look to God and trust in His Word – He strengthens me, imparts His peace, and teaches me more about what it means "to believe in Jesus," rather than trust in my own abilities to sort problems.

The apostle Paul was appointed to be a herald and a teacher of the gospel and in his suffering for doing that – he said of Jesus, "Yet I am not ashamed, because I know whom I have believed, and am convinced that He is able to guard what I have entrusted to Him ..." (2 Timothy 1:12)

God is watching over His word to perform it in our lives, as we believe and "keep believing" in Him.

Believe in Jesus – the One who created you for His purpose

Garden Pond

When we first moved into our home, one of the first garden projects I carried out was to construct a pond. We decided to go for a plastic mould, so from the commencement of digging – I knew the shape and depth of the hole that would be required.

To allow for the deepest part of the pond mould – it needed a depth of 18 inches. As my excavation continued, I came across a problem. With another four inches to dig down, I hit a layer of solid rock!

As a result of that; my pond mould stands a few inches above ground level. Using stones and small pieces of rock that I was able to dig up, I managed to conceal the top of the plastic mould.

Some years later, we tried a different location in the garden for a pond – hoping we may be able to dig deeper before hitting the rock layer. The bad news was – the rock layer was at the same level. The good news is – it is encouraging to know that our home and garden stands on solid rock.

Whatever the state of the ground beneath our feet: God has made it possible for our lives to be founded and grounded, secure and solid in Him. David the psalmist announced "The LORD is my rock, my fortress and my deliverer; my God is my rock in whom I take refuge." (Psalm 18:2a)

Hannah (the mother of Samuel) declared in her prayer to the LORD – "... there is no-one besides you; there is no Rock like our God." (1 Samuel 2:2)

As I look out of my office window, I can observe 3 rocks in Torbay that rise above the currents of the sea and stand strong amidst the crashing waves that come against them. When we seek and follow after Jesus Christ – wo will find Him to be our Rock of safety and shelter in our lives.

Is today, a day of trouble for you? Has your confidence and security been shaken? Has fear stolen your peace of heart and mind?

As we look to God in every circumstance – we can be assured like King David when he declared – "The LORD is the stronghold of my life ... for in the day of trouble He will keep me safe ... and set me high upon a rock." (Psalm 27:1, 5)

God is our rock –
a sure foundation
for our lives

Pilot boat

When I lived in Reading; I used to have a very enjoyable summer job working for the Thames Conservancy – helping to operate the locks on the river. During that time I helped many river craft through the lock system; including canoes, houseboats and Steamers.

One of the vessels I always enjoyed seeing was the high powered and streamlined Conservancy Patrol launch. The Boatmen who transported the River Inspectors around in these boats – navigated and moored their launches with precision, speed and expertise. In contrast; I observed a good number of people (who were probably taking their first boating holiday) experience difficulty, as they did their best to manoeuvre safely on entering a lock!

When I moved to Brixham in the late 70's – I started to enjoy watching the Pilot boats, leaving port and then returning to harbour after helping ships to navigate the waters of Torbay.

What do you do and who do you call upon, when it comes to navigating through the difficult situations and decisions in your life?

Before Jesus returned to His Father in heaven, He said to His disciples that He would not leave them on their own. He promised, "I will ask the Father, and He will give you another Counsellor to be with you for ever –the Spirit of truth." (John 14:16-17)

The Greek word for Counsellor or Comforter is "parakletos" – which means "one called to the side of another to counsel and support" – one called in to help.

Just as a Pilot boat comes alongside a ship to transfer a pilot to give aid and advice – "God; by His Holy Spirit – draws alongside us" – to guard, guide, comfort and help us when we call upon Him, and seek His council.

Jesus is a Pilot for life. He knows the best route for us to take and will lead and direct us as we seek and trust Him. James reminds us "Draw near to God, and He will draw near to you." (James 4:8 ESV Bible)

Paul the apostle gave praise to God when he said "He comes alongside us when we go through hard times" ... (2 Corinthians 1:4 – The Message Bible)

This week: remember that every help, comfort and blessing that God pours out upon us – is given so we can share it with others. Paul went on to say in the above verse ... "and before you know it, He brings us alongside someone else who is going through hard times so that we can be there for that person just as God was there for us."

The Holy Spirit is our Comforter, Counsellor and Guide

Solar eclipse

On Friday 20th March 2015 – millions of people in the UK and northern Europe glimpsed the best solar eclipse in years.

A great path across the Earth's surface was plunged into darkness as the moon came between us and the sun. Like many of us, I was pleased to have seen a short glimpse of the partial eclipse as a small pocket of clear sky formed between the heavy clouds.

I recall viewing the Eclipse of August 11th 1999 from our back garden, when darkness came over Torbay as the shadow of the moon rolled across the earth. Although it was very cloudy and the sun was hardly visible – the speedy effect of rolling darkness and returning to normal light – was an amazing spectacle to witness.

These events reminded me of what the Bible says about the sun and moon, and light and darkness. In Genesis we read – And God said, "Let there be lights in the expanse of the sky to separate the day from the night, and let them serve as signs to mark seasons and days and years, and let them be lights in the expanse of the sky to give light on the earth." And it was so! Genesis 1:14-15)

Everything that we are discovering about the earth, sun moon and stars – has been set in place by God and He holds it all together by His power.

Light and darkness is a big theme in God's Word.

When God sent His Son Jesus to the world, the people walking in darkness saw a great light and on those living in the land of the shadow of death – a light dawned. (Read Isaiah 9:2)

When 'Jesus the light of the world' was crucified (taking away the sins of the world) from the sixth hour until the ninth hour, darkness came over the whole land.

However: God turned the darkness of Good Friday into the glorious light of His resurrection from the dead on Easter Sunday.

Jesus brings light and hope into the darkest situations we may face. If shadows of fear, failure, uncertainty or hopelessness are eclipsing your life today, keep looking to God – 'the darkness will pass and light will return.'

Jesus –
the Light
of the
world

Inspired

The London Marathon usually takes place in April each year. It attracts thousands of entrants and it is the largest annual fundraising event in the world.

I read that in the past, the longest time taken to complete the course was 5 days – by a charity runner wearing a deep-sea diving suit! New regulations (from a few years ago) now state the race must be completed in 1 day.

On many occasions my wife and I have enjoyed watching this run on the TV. Some runners wear amazing outfits – which must make completing the course even more challenging for them.

Most of those taking part have been personally inspired and motivated; to run and raise funds for a charity that has either helped them or a loved one through a difficult time, and this alongside the cheering crowds – can spur them on when the race gets tough.

The Bible tells us that the apostle Paul continually prayed for the Church in Thessalonica when he remembered their "... endurance inspired by hope" in the Lord Jesus. (1 Thessalonians 1:3) The promises from God in his word – will inspire us to keep pressing on through difficult times.

Inspiration is about being mentally stimulated to do something or feel something.

When we live for God – He desires to fulfil every good purpose of ours, and every act prompted by our faith in Him. (See 2 Thessalonians 1:11)

When Paul wrote to Timothy, he reminded him that "All scripture is inspired by God and is useful to teach us what is true and to make us realise what is wrong in our lives. It corrects us when we are wrong and teaches us to do what is right." (2 Timothy 3:16 – New Living Translation)

The God inspired, God breathed, Word of God – helps us make good decisions and leads us in the right direction.

God also wants to inspire us to be creative – for He is the Creator of all things. With our talents and abilities we can serve Him and one another.

Whatever "marathon situation" you may be facing this week – remember that Jesus inspires hope to those who look to Him. He will draw close to you and impart His confidence, assurance and strength – as you run the race of life.

As we run the race of life, Jesus imparts hope and strength to us

What are you looking at?

I used to clean at our local Community College. One day, I was doing some cover cleaning and instead of my usual ground floor location – I was on the top floor. As I pushed the vacuum cleaner around the classrooms – I was able to glimpse the nice sea-view in the distance.

I commented to a teacher: "This is a nice view from up here." The member of staff then pointed out to me the view just below the window. It was the rubbish collection zone – full of wheelie bins – and as I looked, a large black-backed gull was on top of the main skip ready to attack the waste bags!

Despite this; the teacher agreed the sea view was nice, and I said "It is best to look to the horizon!"

I have a similar scenario as I sit in my office writing my thoughts. If I lift my eyes, and look straight ahead out of the window – I see just houses. If I glance slightly left, I look out over miles of sea – with Exmouth and Sidmouth on the horizon.

The Bible is full of examples of people (who without denying their struggles and difficulties) – lifted their eyes from gazing on their problems – and looked to God for His help and solutions.

When the disciple Peter trusted in the call of Jesus to "Come" to Him – he got out of the boat on the storm-tossed lake and started to walk on the water towards Jesus. But when Peter saw the wind, he was afraid and began to sink. (Read the full story in Matthew 14:22-33)

When Peter took his eyes of faith off Jesus and focussed more on his immediate surroundings, he began to sink. The psalmist reminds us to "Look to the Lord and His strength; seek His face always." (Psalm 105:4)

On my journey of faith, I have discovered that God is teaching me more and more about what it means to "fully rely on Him." As I look to Jesus, I may not have immediate answers to all my needs – but I experience His peace and perspective, knowing that in His way and time, He is able to get everything "sorted" – for the best.

Some years ago, I wrote these words as a song. Jesus: "When I call to You, You come to me – You make the storms to cease. You walk out to me, on the troubled sea – and give to me your peace. You are the light on the horizon – the dawning of a brand-new day. The clouds above are passing me by – and You are on your way."

May God fill your heart with hope this week as you look to, and wait on Him. His help is on the way!

Keep your eyes
on Jesus –
The Way, the
Truth and the Life

Destiny

I was encouraged to read about a former dinner lady who had risen through the ranks to become the new Head Teacher of a School.

The 47-year-old lady said, she felt she had "achieved her destiny" after securing the top job at a School in Leighton Buzzard.

She had first volunteered at the school as a parent helper before taking on the role of mid-day supervisor a year later. She began a teaching course while carrying out the supervisor role.

This story made me think about how some people achieve their goals and ambitions through hard work, training and perseverance.

Others may attribute some aspects of their success in life, to fate or chance.

In the Bible, we can discover God's perspective on destiny. It is about His purpose for our lives and what He wants us to be and to become – for today and in the future.

As we read the scriptures, we will see that God desires to use our gifts, skills and resources to fulfil His will for our lives and bring blessing to others.

In the book of Isaiah, we read "I am God, and there is no other; I am God, and there is none like me.

I make known the end from the beginning, from ancient times, what is still to come. I say: My purpose will stand, and I will do all that I please." (Isaiah 46:9-10)

The writer of Hebrews said "May the God of peace ... equip you with everything good for doing His will, and may He work in us what is pleasing to Him, through Jesus Christ ..." (Hebrews 13:20-21)

Reaching our destiny and full potential in God, will involve us obeying and doing what He asks of us in His word – and trusting Him in those times when we feel unequipped and out of our depth.

When it comes to carrying out what God calls us to do: whatever it is, and wherever it may take us – we can draw strength from the promise that Paul gave to the Church in Philippi when he declared – "I have the strength to face all conditions by the power that Christ gives me." (Philippians 4:13 – Good News Bible)

Our days and times are secure in God's strong arms

Be content

When it comes to saving money – there are numerous websites that can 'help us compare' the price we pay for our energy and varied insurance policies – to ensure we get the lowest prices and best features on a product or service. Shopping around for a good deal is fine, and this type of comparison can be beneficial.

However: there is a form of 'comparison' that is not healthy – and it occurs when we compare ourselves to others.

One day while out shopping, I stopped to listen to a street musician. His voice was excellent – and he reminded me of a 'Gary Barlow sound-alike.' I spoke with him and shared my appreciation of his performance.

I haven't got a strong voice; but I love to sing and play guitar, and over the years I have sung in public – both solo and with various bands.

When we compare ourselves to others – it can be easy to think "I wish I had a voice like that." or "If only I had that ability."

God made each of us to be unique. There is no one else like you in the whole world! He has given to us various skills and abilities and He wants us to use these gifts for His glory and purpose – with confidence and assurance.

God wants us to experience the 'joy of being content' with all that we have and are – and not come under the burden that comparison and envy bring.

The apostle Paul wrote to Timothy saying that ..."
godliness with contentment is great gain." (1 Timothy 6:6)

Writing to the Church in Philippi, Paul talks further about aspects of contentment. He explains – "... I have 'learned to be content' whatever the circumstances. I know what it is to be in need, and I know what it is to have plenty. I have 'learned the secret of being content' in any and every situation ... I can do everything through Him (Christ) who gives me strength" (Read Philippians 4:11-13)

This week: I encourage you not to compare yourself to others, but do – what God has enabled only you to do, and may we look for opportunities to share with others the gifts He has imparted to us.

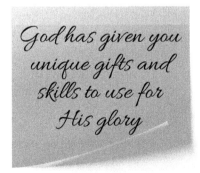

God has given you
unique gifts and
skills to use for
His glory

Garden shed repairs

Our garden shed is home-made. Over the years the main construction has stood firm as strong gales and driving rain have come against it.

One day, I noticed some water had collected on a plastic table that was stored in the middle of the shed.

As I inspected the roof above it, I noticed that the boards were damp. I had often seen magpies and seagulls taking their food scraps to eat on the roof and wondered if they had pecked small holes in the felt, which were now allowing rain to penetrate.

Around the same time, I discovered that in one of the corners of the shed – the floor would sag as I stood on it. Damp had entered in at the base, and some of the boarding was beginning to fall apart.

We took our shed through a 'renewing process' as we had the roof re-felted and new boarding put down for the floor. It was now restored to its former strength and condition!

As we go through life – we will all enter those seasons when we feel that need to be refreshed and renewed.

We are looking for hope and purpose in the mundane and strength to keep going when things around us fail or disappoint us.

God's word – the Bible, can bring renewal into our lives. The psalmist prayed "... renew my life according to your word ... teach me your decrees." (Read Psalm 119:25-26)

Reading scripture renews our thinking and helps us understand God's purpose and perspective in all that we are going through.

Isaiah the prophet reminds us that "... those who hope in the Lord will renew their strength." (Isaiah 40:31) God gives His strength to the weary.

The apostle Paul experienced the renewing power and presence of God in his life. As he shared the message of the gospel – he had been hard pressed on every side – not sure of what to do at times, persecuted and had been thrown down.

However: he went on to say – "We do not lose heart. Though outwardly we are wasting away, yet inwardly we are being renewed day by day." (2 Corinthians 4:7-9, 16)

As we read and trust in God's Word – we will find peace, hope, faith and grace that will be sufficient for each day.

God renews us with His grace and strength

Replacement printer

I was looking to purchase a new printer for our computer system. Our old model had served us well for over five years until a message on screen requested we "Contact the Service Centre." We soon discovered it would be cheaper to purchase a new printer than repair the old one.

To my surprise and delight, I found a new printer cost me less than what I had paid for the old model, and it also had many more features including Wi-Fi connection, Scanner and photo-copy facility. (I've just got to learn how to use them all now!)

It is always good when products and services exceed our expectations. I was reading some holiday destination reviews on a web-site where one comment read "It was 'more than' we could have hoped for!"

This brought to my mind how God is a generous and bountiful God. He gives to us in great measure, things that will accomplish His will in our lives. He imparts to us 'immeasurably more' than all we could ask for or imagine. (Ephesians 3:20)

On the top of the pages of my prayer journal, I write "What impossible things am I praying for?" It reminds me that God wants to accomplish so much more than my mind can comprehend. Nothing is too difficult for the LORD.

Jesus said "If you, then, though you are evil, know how to give good gifts to your children, 'how much more' will your Father in heaven give good gifts to those who ask Him." (Matthew 7:11)

There will always be something more that God wants to teach us, and somewhere new where He wants to use us in serving Him and others.

Paul reminded the believers in Rome that trouble, hardship, persecution and danger ... could not separate them from the love of Christ.

He added "... in all these things we are 'more than conquerors' through Him who loved us." (Read Romans 8:35-39)

As we seek and ask of God, He imparts His faithful love, amazing grace and endless blessings into our lives in abundance. He gives us 'more' – so that we can pass it on to others.

The apostle Paul put it like this – "God can bless you with everything you need, and you will always have more than enough to do all kinds of good things for others." (2 Corinthians 9:8 – Contemporary English Version)

God is able to do more than we could ask or imagine

Life changing Book

We were taking a few days holiday in the City of Bath. During a time of 'checking out the retail outlets' – my wife and I discovered a large Bookshop which had a huge choice of titles. We did not have the time to browse all the shelves and tables of stock.

I always enjoy looking at the non-fiction books. If you want to learn how to cook, mend your car, build a garden patio, play piano or maintain your property – there are plenty of books that will give you the 'know how.' For those who prefer fiction – there will always be the latest romantic, crime or mystery novels to read.

In my 'Thought for the Week' writing, I make regular mention of God's Word, the Bible, which is still the world's best-selling and widely distributed book. The Bible was written by men but inspired by God. "All scripture is God-breathed and is useful for teaching, rebuking, correcting and training in righteousness ..." (2 Timothy 3:16) The Bible equips us for every good work.

An 'autobiography' book will tell us all about the writers' life, but for most of us it is un-likely we will ever meet or know the author in person.

However: when it comes to the Bible – the scriptures not only tell us about God, but through His story – He wants to make himself known to the reader personally. God's Son Jesus is the 'Author of life' (See Acts 3:15)

The Bible was not written just for knowledge and information. Jesus said "You search the Scriptures because you think they will give you eternal life. But the Scriptures 'point to Me' (John 5:39 – New Living Translation)

Concerning the purpose of the Bible; John wrote in his gospel –"Jesus did many other miraculous signs in the presence of His disciples, which are not recorded in this book. But these are written that you may believe that Jesus is the Christ, the Son of God, and that by believing you may have life in His name." (John 20:30-31)

John explained further saying – Jesus did many other things; and if every one of them were written down, the whole world would not have room for the books that would be written. (See John 21:25)

If you have a Bible on your bookshelf – you possess a powerful and 'life changing book' – where God longs to make His love and purposes known as you read His story 'written for you!'

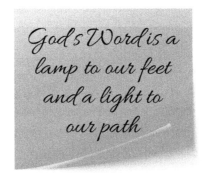

God's Word is a lamp to our feet and a light to our path

How are you today?

When I meet someone I know, I often use the greeting – "How has your week been?" By asking this question, they can tell me what they've been doing or tell me how they feel.

I have come to realise, if we are to genuinely ask someone 'how they are' we need to be prepared to give them time and a listening ear for their answer.

I read about the following actual conversation, heard by a student in a dining hall. "How are you?" – "Good. You?" – "Pretty good." – "That's good."

There will be times when we don't want to go into detail and share with others about how we are feeling (or open-up about the problems we are experiencing) but there may be occasions when we are desperate for someone to care and come alongside us, and we long for a person to show interest in us.

The Bible reveals; God is fully aware how each of us feels, without us saying a word. David the Psalmist proclaimed "O Lord, You have searched me and 'known me!' You 'know' when I sit down and when I rise up; You 'discern' my thoughts from afar. You search out my path and my lying down and are 'acquainted with all my ways.' Even before a word is on my tongue, behold, O Lord You 'know it' altogether." (Psalm 139:1-4 – English Standard Version)

God is interested in each of us – and everything about our lives, and is ready to listen when we call upon Him.

"As a father has compassion on his children, so the Lord has compassion on those who fear Him; for He knows how we are formed ... "(Psalm 103:13-14) God is all knowing – concerning how your day is going.

The prophet Isaiah tells us that 'Jesus was familiar with suffering.' He understands about being despised and rejected. He took up our infirmities and carried our sorrows. (Read Isaiah 53:3-5) Whatever we are going through, we can cast our cares and anxieties on God because He cares for us.

The Bible tells us to 'count others more significant than ourselves' and to 'look not only to our own interests, but also to the interests of others'. (Philippians 2:4)

This week, as we ask others "How are you?" – we may get to understand 'how they really are' as we make time to listen carefully to them.

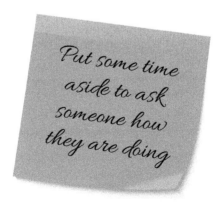

Put some time aside to ask someone how they are doing

Watch your blind spot

After passing my driving test (aged 17) the first car I purchased was a Mini. Sadly; I only owned it for 2 years – because after colliding with a 'Rolls Royce' – my car was written off!

The accident occurred in a busy, three lane, unmarked road. I had indicated to move right – but I obviously didn't check my blind spot before moving over.

Recently when walking along a road; I observed a lorry, and then heard an automated voice announce repeatedly, "Stand well clear – vehicle reversing!" All drivers need to be alert to the possible blind spots that occur when manoeuvring.

We can also have 'blind-spots' in certain areas of our lives when we cannot see properly. We may hit a blind-spot when our opinion on something is obstructed by either the 'lack of understanding or impartiality.' Prejudice can stop us seeing people as they really are.

The Bible makes many references to how we need others to watch out for us. (It usually takes another person to inform you that the rear light on your car is not working!)

If I take on a leadership role, I choose someone to become my 'accountability person' at meetings – who I ask to watch out for my blind-spots. I invite them to let me know if they think I've spoken in an inappropriate manner or responded with a wrong attitude.

The Bible says –"The way of a fool seems right to him, but a wise man listens to advice." (Proverbs 12:15) Another proverb reads "As iron sharpens iron, so one man sharpens another." (Proverbs 27:17)

Over the years, I have appreciated the input of friends sharing God's Word with me – reminding and enabling me to see God's perspective for situations in my life.

Paul the apostle wrote, "Let the Word of Christ dwell in you richly as you 'teach and admonish one another' with all wisdom ..." (Colossians 3:16)

When you meet with a close friend this week – remember "Two people are better than one for they can help each other succeed. If one person falls, the other can reach out and help. But someone who falls alone is in real trouble." (Ecclesiastes 4:9-10 – New Living Translation)

A wise person
will listen
to advice

Learning zone

At the College where I used to work, there was a poster on one of the doors of the Learning Resource Centre which read "You are about to enter a Learning Zone!"

As the years go by, I become increasingly aware of how much I still have to learn and the need to 'remain teachable.'

When it comes to guitar playing; I know regular practice, and watching or playing with other musicians, is the only way I will improve my skills on the instrument.

All learning takes time and determined effort. Throughout life, we will all learn new skills, either by practice or being taught by others and also accumulate knowledge about many different things.

In addition to the gifts and abilities God imparts to us – the Bible reveals He desires to teach, lead and guide us through every decision and circumstance in life. Each day (with its challenges and responsibilities) is a 'learning zone.'

Isaiah the prophet declared this promise from God – "I am the LORD your God, who teaches you what is best for you, who directs you in the way you should go." (Isaiah 48:18)

God teaches us 'how to experience life to the full' as we put our trust in Him. The psalmist acknowledged, "Since my youth, O God, You have taught me, and to this day I declare your marvellous deeds." (Psalm 71:17)

When I'm preaching I often say, "What will we do as a result of what we've heard today?" If we don't put into action what God asks of us – it will become just information – but if we practice what the Bible says, it becomes our learning experience and we will continue to grow in our faith.

God is patient, loving and merciful as we learn to trust Him. Some lessons in life take longer than others. The apostle Paul said he had 'learned to be content' in any and every situation.

Paul 'learnt about the spiritual discipline of contentment' through many seasons of his life – when he was in need, or living with plenty, being well fed but at times going hungry. (See Philippians 4:11-12)

He also learnt 'Christ; would grant him strength to do all things – in the good times, but also in his troubles. Jesus will do the same for us – as we choose to obey what He teaches in His Word.

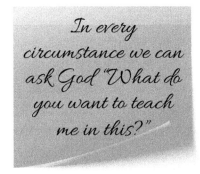

In every circumstance we can ask God "What do you want to teach me in this?"

Paint brushes

For a good number of years, I cleaned the Art block at the local College. As I went around the rooms, I frequently observed brushes which had become hardened with paint or glue.

When I'm decorating at home, I often find my brushes have hardened from not being thoroughly cleaned after their last use.

Just as paint remains in brushes and causes them to harden, it can serve to remind us of the need to guard against those things that may cause us to become 'hard hearted' – making us insensitive and unsympathetic in our attitudes and actions.

We can become hard-hearted when we start to take things for granted – when it becomes easier to grumble and complain rather than express appreciation, and when our glass appears half empty rather than half full. The Bible warns "...he who hardens his heart falls into trouble." (Proverbs 29:14)

We need to keep watch for the signs and symptoms of our hearts becoming hard. 'Heart hardening' can also set in when we stop believing the best about people, and when we only see the bad and negative in situations instead of looking for the good. God reminds us; love bears all things, believes all things, hopes all things and endures all things. (1 Corinthians 13:7)

The writer of Hebrews says of God: "Today, if you hear His voice, 'do not harden your hearts' as you did in the rebellion, during the time of testing in the desert, where your fathers tested and tried me"... (See Hebrews 3:7-10)

The people became hard-hearted when they doubted and disobeyed the Lord. Their hearts had gone astray as they did not know God's ways.

The apostle Paul instructed the Church at Ephesus to "Be kind to one another, tender hearted, forgiving one another, as God in Christ forgave you." (Ephesians 4:32)

The amazing kindness and compassion that we receive from God enables us to remain tender hearted in all circumstances and in all our relationships.

Only God
can change
the human
heart

A first time for everything

On the 7th July 2013, Andy Murray won the Men's Wimbledon Tennis Championship, becoming the first British man to do so since Fred Perry in 1936.

One year later, Murray returned to the scene of his triumph and commented on the pressure of defending his title. He told BBC Sport, "I don't know how I'm going to handle the situation; no one does ... it will be interesting for me to see how I deal with it."

Doing something for the first time can be scary as we face the unknown.

Some years ago, I recall stopping at traffic lights on my motorcycle and being asked for a lift by another biker who had broken down. I managed to take him the 5 miles to his destination – but I didn't mention to him I hadn't ridden with a passenger before! (I wonder if he would have accepted the lift if he had known?) This 'first time experience' gave me the confidence that I could do it again.

This reminded me of the story in the Bible when Jesus was walking on the lake (during a storm) to meet his disciples. They were terrified – thinking they had seen a ghost. Peter said, "Lord, if it's you, tell me to come to you on the water." Jesus replied "Come" and Peter stepped out of the boat. (Read the full story and outcome in Matthew 14:22-33) This was certainly a first-time experience for Peter!

As children are growing up, they 'learn to do something for the first time' most days.

As we get older, it can be easier to conform to our routines and retreat to our comfort zones and places of security. When we do, we miss the opportunity to grow and learn.

As we follow God's way (as we put our faith in His words of promise) He will enable us to have courage, confidence and ability as we face and tackle tasks that we have not encountered before.

When King Jehoshaphat sought the Lord he prayed, "We do not know what to do, but our eyes are upon You." (2 Chronicles 20:12)

Being asked by God (or others) to do something for the first time will be a huge challenge to us. We will be walking rocky roads and treading unfamiliar paths.

However: the writer of Hebrews reminds us, the God of peace will 'equip you with everything good for doing His will' and 'works in us' what is pleasing to Him. (Hebrews 13:20-21)

If you face a 'first time' situation this week: trust God, and remember the words that Paul wrote to Timothy saying, "... God has not given us a spirit of fear, but of power and of love and of a sound mind." (2 Timothy 1:7 New King James Bible)

When you don't know what to do – Keep your eyes on Jesus

Good and bad

While looking through a magazine, I read "Have you got an invaluable tip? Don't keep it to yourself!" One simple suggestion was, "Try using the inside of a banana's peel to polish leather shoes – the oils and potassium are great for adding shine and preserving the quality of the material."

I haven't tried this yet, but if it works, it is certainly a good benefit compared to the bad aspect of banana skins – where some people have slipped-up on them!

This got me thinking about other things, which can be both good and bad.

Exposure to the sun can produce vitamin D in our bodies which is necessary to absorb calcium and form healthy bones – but the sun's ultraviolet rays can also burn and damage our skin. The caffeine (in our coffee) has benefits and disadvantages.

The 'Internet' gives access to a host of resources and information; both good and beneficial but also bad and destructive.

James (the brother of Jesus) made comment about this subject of 'good and bad' with reference to the use of our tongues. He commented, "With the tongue we praise our Lord and Father, and with it we curse men, who have been made in God's likeness. 'Out of the same mouth come praise and cursing.' My brothers, this should not be." (James 3:9-10)

There are other things in life which are good or bad – not both. Daily, we will face decisions and dilemmas – and the choices we make will lead to either a good outcome or a bad one.

The writer of Psalm 119 prayed to the Lord saying, "May your hand be ready to help me, for I have chosen your precepts." (verse 173)

When we acknowledge God in every situation, He is willing and able to lead and guide us – not just on a good path – but the 'best path' for our lives.

God wants all things to work for our good – for He alone is good – and what He does is good.

King David declared, "The Lord is good to all; He has compassion on all He has made." (Psalm 145:9)

This week – if you come across something which can be used or seen in either a good or bad way, let it serve as a reminder of the words of Paul when he said, "Don't let evil get the best of you; get the best of evil by doing good." (Romans 12:21 –The Message Bible)

Let us not grow weary of doing good, for in due season we will reap ...

A question of scruples

I was looking at some board games for sale in a Charity shop and came across one called 'A Question of Scruples.' This is a game based on ethical dilemmas –where your friends (the other players) are the Jury – and they have to decide if you are telling the truth or bluffing – in response to the questions asked about what you would do in certain situations.

One example on the back of the game box read – "... you accidentally damage a car in a parking lot, do you leave a note with your name and phone number on?"

Some years ago on the news, they reported the outcome of a social experiment carried out in Manchester to test the honesty and generosity of the City's residents.

Five, £5 notes were pinned to a board with the wording "This money is for people in need only." Many took photos with no-one touching the free money. Two women were seen removing 2 of the notes, but this was so they could hand it to a nearby homeless man.

One man pinned an extra £5 note to the board, while in contrast – two other men took the remaining money, and when they were challenged they just laughed and walked away.

Honesty involves truthfulness, integrity, fairness and sincerity. The Bible calls us to 'speak the truth from our heart.' (Psalm 15:2) Proverbs 24:26 tells us, "An honest answer is like a kiss on the lips."

When Jesus was praying for His disciples He said, "Father ... make them holy in the truth, your word is truth." (John 17:17 – New Living Translation)

Jesus is the way, the truth and the life – He modelled truth in His every word and deed – and as we follow Him and live according to His word, He will grant strength and power to enable us to 'walk in truthfulness.'

The psalmist declared "I have 'chosen' the way of truth ..." (Psalm 119:30) When we don't have 'fixed principles' in life, we can be doubtful or hesitant about what is the right thing to do when we face difficult or tempting situations.

When we choose to set our values and principles according to what the Bible says, we will 'know the best course of action' in every circumstance – and experience the blessing and peace of mind that Jesus gives to those who 'put His Word into practice.'

Choose and walk the pathway of truth

28

Come as you are

I always enjoy watching the Wimbledon Lawn Tennis Championship on TV – and in recent years before the tournament commences, the BBC have used various trailers to promote their coverage of matches. I recall one year, when the footage showed Wimbledon scenes, outlining rules and regulations that both competitors and spectators were asked to adhere to.

"Competitors must be dressed in suitable white tennis attire that is almost entirely white. White does not include off-white or cream. All members of the crowd are politely reminded that they must remain perfectly silent for the duration of every point. In addition, common standards of decency are required at all times."

The pictures and commentary (from current Wimbledon clips) portrayed the opposites of these requests; showing a colourfully dressed crowd, with the players and those watching, jumping and shouting for joy when points were won! The trailer concluded with the words – "Come as you are!"

'Come as you are' is a wonderful invitation – to be yourself – to be accepted for who you are, how you are and where you are – in your journey of life.

It is in this setting of 'as we are' that Jesus calls us to follow Him. When Jesus called some fishermen to be his first disciples they left their nets, boat and family 'at once' – to follow Jesus. (Read Matthew 4:18-22)

They came as they were – and as they heeded the example and words of Jesus, their lives were changed as they learnt to live life the way God intended. At times their lives were turned upside-down through the challenges of discipleship. However, as they obeyed Jesus – they experienced His favour, peace and blessing.

The well-known hymn writer Horatius Bonar wrote the words –"I came to Jesus as I was, weary, and worn and sad; I found in him a resting-place, and He has made me glad."

Whatever our past may hold over us and whatever the future has in store for us; we can come to God as we are – in our need, with our problems, in our sinfulness and brokenness. Jesus said, "...whoever comes to me I will never drive away." (John 6:37)

God doesn't wait for us to be good enough before He calls us to follow Him. He demonstrates His amazing grace and love in that 'while we were still sinners' – He sent His son Jesus to die for us. (so we could know God's forgiveness) See Romans 5:8.

We come as we are and as we trust 'in Christ' – we are a new creation; the old has gone, the new has come!" (2 Corinthians 5:17)

Jesus calls to each of us and says – "Follow Me"

29

Games Court lines

When I was an Exam Invigilator, most of the exams at the College where I worked were held in the Sports Hall. The floor was marked up as a Games Court, and as I walked around invigilating, I could see the various coloured lines for the different sports that could be played in the hall – including 5 a-side football, basketball, netball and badminton.

As I observed these, I was reminded of the importance of lines on courts and pitches.

Could you imagine playing a game of football or badminton without them? Rules bring order and fairness into what would be chaos if there were no boundaries.

I read, "A game is only as good as its 'rules' and how well we play the game is defined by how well we follow the rules... Rules are what actually define what the game is."

The Bible is God's Word; that speaks order, purpose, perspective and justice into every situation. The 10 Commandments (that God gave through Moses) consist of 4 commands about our relationship with God, and 6 concerning how we live and relate with others.

These rules were not given to restrict us – but to 'protect us' – so our lives don't become broken and disordered as a result of our sinfulness.

When Jesus delivered His Sermon on the Mount, (Matthew 5:3–7:27) He gave many commands and boundaries to help us live our lives to the full; pleasing to God and a blessing to others, and just like in any sport or game we play, 'if we don't follow the rules – we won't benefit!'

As we face decisions and choices in life, we need to bring God's precepts alongside our every word, action and motive and 'live in the light of what God asks of us.' When we acknowledge the Lord – He makes our paths straight. (Proverbs 3:6)

Jesus said, "If you love me, you will obey what I command." (John 14:15) This is mentioned again in the letter of 1 John 5:3 when the writer says, "Loving God means keeping His commandments, and His commandments are not burdensome."

God's commandments are not burdensome because they are always full of grace and truth, and always for our good. The psalmist wrote, "Because I love your commands more than gold, more than pure gold, and because 'I consider all your precepts right,' I hate every wrong path. (Psalm 119:127-128)

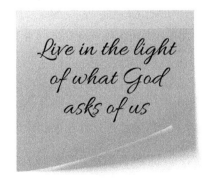
Live in the light
of what God
asks of us

You're covered

I was waiting to be served in my local bank when I noticed a promotional flyer in a dispenser. The words on the cover read – "Relax. You're covered."

The leaflet outlined the additional benefits on a graduate account to cover against loss or theft of a mobile phone, bank cards, passport or driving licence.

When we receive our insurance renewal documents there are several pages highlighting 'what is covered' and 'not covered' under the policy. Regardless of how much insurance we may choose to take out, it can never cover us totally against every unforeseen or unwanted occurrence in life.

The Bible addresses this theme of 'being covered.' The Good News of the gospel is God sent his Son Jesus to cover our sinfulness by his forgiveness. Jesus ... himself bore our sins in His body on the tree (cross) so that we might die to sins and live for righteousness ... (1 Peter 2:24)

Paul the apostle proclaimed, "Blessed are they whose transgressions are forgiven, whose 'sins are covered.' Blessed is the man whose sin the Lord will never count against him." (Romans 4:7-8) When God forgives sins – He remembers them no more!

If we confess our sins, God is faithful and just and will forgive us our sins and purify us from all unrighteousness.

The love of Christ, and the sacrifice of Christ on the cross has also 'covered us' from having to live in the brokenness, guilt and shame that sin brings into our lives.

Isaiah the prophet said of the Lord, "He has clothed me with the garments of salvation; He has 'covered me' with the robe of righteousness ... (Isaiah 61:10 – English Standard Version)

The psalmist spoke of another aspect of God's keeping and protection when he said of the Lord – "He will cover you with His feathers, and under His wings you will find refuge ... (Psalm 91:4) Just as a bird shelters its young under their wings – so God covers us.

You may be going through a hard time this week where you need to know you are 'covered by God's love, comfort and mercy'. Come under the shelter of His wings – rest in the shadow of the Almighty. There is room for everyone.

When God forgives sins – He remembers them no more

Broken jug

I heard on the news some years ago, Museum staff from a Mansion in Ipswich were trying to find a little boy who was 'devastated' after accidentally smashing a historic jug.

The staff wanted the boy to know the 18th Century Delftware puzzle jug he knocked off a window ledge (some time ago) 'had been fixed.' Thanks to a Conservation Officer's efforts, each of the 65 pieces it broke into had been painstakingly glued.

I can recall occasions as a young boy, the disappointment experienced when some of my favourite toys broke. Beyond repair; I had to face the fact, the 'joy of play' they once offered – was no more.

As life goes on, brokenness with material things continues. The washing machine leaks, the freezer defrosts – even when switched on, the shower fails, and the car breaks down. (hopefully not all on the same day!)

These things are replaceable – but what do we do when our hearts and lives get broken? – when people break their promises made to us – when all hope is lost, trust is shattered and misunderstanding divides.

It has been said, "God will mend a broken heart if you give Him all the pieces." David the Psalmist shares about his brokenness in Psalm 31.

He speaks of his affliction, distress, anguish and sorrow. His strength had failed and he was a 'dread to his friends' – even forgotten by them as though dead.

David said "I have become like broken pottery." (Psalm 31:12) In his need, David put his trust in the Lord – because he knew God held every moment and circumstance of his life – in His strong hands.

Another psalmist gave praise to the Lord saying, "He heals the broken-hearted and binds up their wounds." (Psalm 147:3) The prophet Isaiah spoke of the Lord as the One who was anointed to preach the good news ... and 'sent to bind up the broken-hearted'... (Isaiah 61:1)

God longs for us to know He is the fixer of broken hearts and lives. "The Lord is close to the broken-hearted and saves those who are crushed in spirit ..." (Psalm 34:18)

When we make God our refuge – we will know His healing love and touch restoring us. David the psalmist experienced this. He said "At day's end I'm ready for sound sleep, For You, God, have put my life back together." (Psalm 4:8 – The Message Bible)

God is the fixer of broken hearts

Mind the wasps

My wife and I went on a day trip to Shaldon and Teignmouth. Before taking the passenger ferry across the estuary we decided to have a coffee and croissant in a Cafe in Shaldon. It was a perfect summer day – so we chose to sit in the outside seating area so we could enjoy the lovely surroundings.

Within seconds of the drinks and pastries arriving at our table; numerous wasps appeared – making their way onto the jam, marmalade and butter pots.

We were impressed by a mother (who was sitting at a nearby table) who remained very calm and confident as wasps landed on their meals. As a result, her young children were not overly alarmed by the wasps arrival.

As we try to fend wasps away from our sweet foods – we fear they will retaliate by giving us a 'painful sting.' It is the female wasps that have the stinger which is able to deliver multiple stings.

I ate my croissant quickly (with only a little jam) but enjoyed my coffee after the preserves had been removed from the table by the waitress.

This incident made me think about the circumstances in life that can deliver a sting to us – causing harm, discomfort, anxiety and emotional pain.

In the Bible we read about Job who experienced stings of great loss, misery and turmoil. While experiencing these, his consolation and joy in 'unrelenting pain' was that he had not denied the words of the Holy One. (See Job 6:10)

God's Word will always sustain us throughout the dark and painful seasons in life – bringing hope, revealing perspective and giving purpose to every situation.

David the Psalmist sought God's help when things got difficult for him. When he encountered the stings of pain and distress he prayed, "May your salvation, O God, protect me." (See Psalm 69:29)

Speaking about the hope of the 'resurrection of the body'– Paul the apostle proclaims "Death has been swallowed up in victory. Where, O death, is your victory? Where, O death, is your sting?"(1 Corinthians 15:54-55)

When God raised His Son Jesus from the dead, He accomplished for us – the best 'sting removal' – the world could ever know. For those who put their trust in Jesus and follow Him – 'the fear and sting of death itself' – is removed. In and with Christ alone, we have the hope of abundant life on earth and eternal life in heaven.

In every pain or sting we may experience, or whatever may come against us – be encouraged by the promise; that 'nothing in all creation' can separate us from the love of God that is in Christ Jesus.

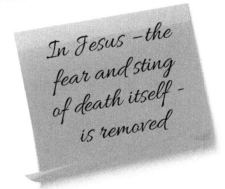

In Jesus – the fear and sting of death itself – is removed

Close encounter

On the 15th July 2015, a signal received from the New Horizons Spacecraft showed it had survived its historic encounter with Pluto. The data suggested the spacecraft experienced no upsets as it hurtled past the icy world at a speed of 31,000 miles per hour.

On that day, the message that came through a giant dish in Madrid, Spain – 'took 4 hours and 25 minutes to traverse 4.7 billion km of space!'

When I read statistics like this, it reminds me just how vast the universe is. It is amazing we have the skills and technology to send a spacecraft that distance and be able to send pictures of Pluto back to earth.

However; even more awesome is the fact – the vastness of the universe was formed at God's command – and 'He is in it all.'

Isaiah the prophet refers to the Lord God as the Creator of the 'ends of the earth.' The Lord Himself declares "Do I not fill heaven and earth?" (Jeremiah 23:24)

Solomon said of God "The heavens, even the highest heaven, cannot contain you." (1 Kings 8:27)

As King David pondered on the majesty and power of God in creation – He asked this question of the Lord. "When I consider your heavens, the work of your fingers, the moon and the stars, which You have set in place, what is man that you are mindful of him ... that you care for him?" (Psalm 8:3-4)

The thought behind this question is: in the big picture of life – "How can we be of such importance and significance to God, and worthy of His attention?"

In your 'small corner' – wherever you live and whatever you are facing, the God who fills the entire universe is not distant from you. Maybe your circumstances make you feel like God is millions of miles away. However, "The Lord is near to all who call on Him ... in truth." (Psalm 145:18)

This week, you may find yourself gazing into a 'sky full of stars.' (or clouds) Next time you do, remember – the God who brings forth the constellations in their seasons, knows the laws of the heavens and has wisdom to count the clouds – is mindful of you! (Read Job 38:31-37)

Through looking to Jesus, we can personally know the Creator of creation. "For by (Jesus Christ) all things were created, things in heaven and on earth ...and 'in Him' all things hold together." (Colossians 1:16-17) The grace, help and strength of Jesus is only a prayer away.

God who fills the entire universe is not distant from you

Consumers and Contributors

On 1st October 2015 the new 'Consumer Rights Act' came into force, and all purchases we make as consumers from this date onwards will be governed by this legislation. It gives new 'consumer protection' measures and for the first time anyone who buys faulty goods will be entitled to a full refund for up to 30 days after the purchase. The Act also gives protection for people who buy digital content such as on-line films and music.

It is good and assuring to know – we can be protected as 'consumers' by these new rights and measures.

As I thought on the benefits of this new Act, it made me appreciate how much we have as 'consumers in society.' Our supermarket shelves are stacked with choice and abundant stocks of food, drink and other commodities. We have easy access to resources, goods and services covered by satisfaction guarantees – and some retailers may refund or exchange goods – even if you 'change your mind' about a purchase.

The Bible reminds us, we also have a responsibility to be 'contributors' to our communities for their blessing – and to the wider world.

The writer of the book of Hebrews tells us, "... Do not neglect to do good and to share what you have, for such sacrifices are pleasing to God." (Hebrews 13:16)

Sharing and contributing into the lives of others is sacrificial, because it will cost us time, resources and commitment.

As a consumer we take and use – as a contributor we give and bless others. Jesus himself said, "It is more blessed to give than to receive." (Acts 20:35)

God blesses us, so we can be generous hearted in giving to those in need. "Generous hands are blessed hands, because they give bread to the poor." (Proverbs 22:9 – The Message Bible)

Another time Jesus shared with His disciples saying "Give, and it will be given to you ... for the measure you use, it will be measured to you." (Read Luke 6:37-38)

This week we will all need to be consumers – but we will also have opportunity to contribute something back into our communities and the lives of people we meet.

We contribute 'God qualities' – when we live in peace with each other ... encourage the timid, help the weak, be patient with everyone ... don't pay back wrong for wrong and always try to be kind to everyone ... (See 1 Thessalonians 5:13-15)

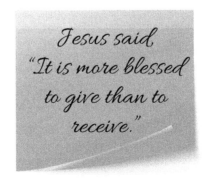

Jesus said,
"It is more blessed
to give than to
receive."

Remembering and forgetting

We all experience those moments when we forget things and we ask: Where did I put the car keys? What did I come upstairs for? What time did we agree to meet?

In our culture of technology – it can be 'easy to forget a password' that enables us to access on-line services, or we get a 'blank mind' at the shop till when we are asked to enter our pin number when paying by card.

We also have those 2 occasions each year when we have to remember the dates to change the clocks – putting them 'forward one hour in the spring' and 'back one hour in winter time.'

Moments of forgetfulness can become a little more difficult when it involves another person and not just ourselves. This can happen if we overlook to send a birthday or anniversary card to a family member or friend – or 'forget a person's name!'

In the Bible, there is a wonderful promise that God makes. He declares to His people "... I will not forget you! See, I have engraved you on the palms of my hands ..." (Isaiah 49:14)

At times we may feel forsaken and forgotten, but as we turn to God and trust in Him – we will know His comfort and compassion and we can be confident knowing our times (and our names) are in His hands.

The psalmist wrote, "The Lord remembers us and will bless us..." (Psalm 115:12)

The Lord remembers us – and we are to remember Him. Throughout the pages of the Bible, God said to His people – "Remember how the Lord your God led you – remember all the commands of the Lord – the wonders He has done, and remember the words of the Lord Jesus..."

Interestingly: God's word also tells us about a few things that are useful to forget. Isaiah the prophet said, "Forget the former things; do not dwell on the past. See, I am doing a new thing!" (Isaiah 43:18) God wants to accomplish new things in our lives that will be a blessing to Him and to others.

If we are living with the burden from bad choices and decisions we have made in the past – when we confess our sins to God, He says He will forgive us and 'remember our sins no more.'(See Jeremiah 31:34b) In Christ – we are made new and have a fresh start.

Paul the apostle also said, "One thing I do: 'forgetting what lies behind' and straining forward to what lies ahead, I press on toward the goal for the prize of the upward call of God in Christ Jesus. (Philippians 3:13)

Paul forgot the lesser things from the past, and remembered to keep his eyes fixed on the greater things for the future. Let us remember to do the same!

Remember the wonders that God has done

36

Salt or no salt?

One lunch-time, I opened my usual brand of 'ready salted' crisps to enjoy. After eating a few, I realised that something was different. The crisps were not salty!

Being in a multi-pack we ended up having to eat 12 packs of crisps (not on the same day) which must have missed the 'salting process.' It was good when I was able to savour again the 'saltiness' in this popular snack.

Although too much salt is not good for our health – it is vital for life. Salt maintains the correct balance of certain fluids (which bathes the cells in our bodies) essential for nerve and muscle function.

Salt seasons; and makes things taste better and salt preserves, to prevent decay.

Jesus made reference to salt when He taught his disciples – as He shared his Sermon on the Mount. He said, "You are the salt of the earth ..." (Matthew 5:13)

Those first disciples would have understood the function of salt. The fish they caught (without refrigeration) would soon spoil unless protected and packed in salt.

The Message Bible says, "Let me tell you why you are here. You're here to be salt-seasoning that brings out the God flavours of this earth. If you lose your saltiness, how will people taste godliness?"

Mark records in his gospel, that Jesus said, "Salt is good, but if it loses its saltiness, how can you make it salty again? Have salt in yourselves, and be at peace with each other." (Mark 9:50)

Our lives remain 'salted' when we obey what God asks of us in His word; live in right relationship with Him – and one another – and as we seek to live our lives that will point others towards Jesus and His ways.

It is not just our actions that need to be 'seasoned with salt' but our 'words' also. Paul the apostle said, "Let your conversation be always full of grace, seasoned with salt, so that you may know how to answer everyone." (Colossians 4:6)

Followers of Jesus are to be both 'salt and light' in the world. (Matthew 5:13-16) He wants to use our lives, so people around can 'taste and see' what God is like. In our communities and among family and friends, we are that 'small amount of salt' that can make a huge difference, and make life 'taste better' for those in need.

This week: let us choose to 'add salt seasoning' into people's lives as we find ways of sharing and speaking about – God's forgiveness, goodness, love, and kindness.

You are here to be salt-seasoning that brings out the God flavours of this earth

Without blemish

In September 1999, we took possession of the best 'second-hand car' we have ever owned. We bought from a friend – a Volkswagen Polo – which was 17 years old and only had 7000 miles on the clock. It had been kept in a garage, regularly serviced and the paintwork was immaculate, with no signs of any rust. When you opened the doors, there was still a hint of the pleasant smell you get from upholstery when it is new.

It would have been good to have continued to keep this car as a 'collector's item' – but we had purchased it for practical purposes and I used it to transport my market stall goods.

I remember the day when we discovered the first small dent and chipped paintwork on one of the doors. (possibly caused by a shopping trolley in a car-park) We used touch up paint over the bare metal – but our 'good as new' car had now received its first blemish. Others followed!

More recently, I noticed on our reasonably new, white garage door – small rust spots beginning to appear. On contacting the manufacturer, they sent me some cream and paint to cover them over.

Most of us can recall experiences when something new or precious to us has been spoiled by being dented or blemished. In the bible we read; how in the beginning, God created Adam and Eve – perfect and flawless – because they were without sin.

As they chose to do their own thing and disobey what God commanded them, their 'sin blemished' lives made them feel afraid and ashamed and they hid from God in their nakedness. (Read the full story in Genesis chapter 3)

Jesus is God's remedy for us – against the damage and spoiling that our sin, wrong choices and disobedience has caused in our lives.

The 'forgiveness' we can receive in Jesus when we ask of Him – covers our sinfulness. Just as Adam and Eve were 'clothed by God' after their fall (Genesis 3:21) 'Jesus covers and clothes us with His righteousness' so we can live in right-standing with God.

This is the hope we have for the things that have put a spot and blemish upon our lives. Jesus came, so that out of His great love for His Church ('everyone' who believes in Him) He would present them – "to himself as a radiant church, without stain or wrinkle or any other blemish, but holy and blameless." (Ephesians 5:27)

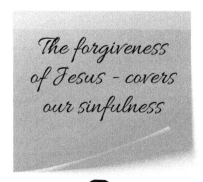

The forgiveness of Jesus - covers our sinfulness

Want or need?

During a shopping trip, my wife and I treated ourselves to a cup of tea and some cake in a Cafe. I collected some paper serviettes from the end of the serving counter and on them I found written this challenging four-line poem.

"Napkins are made from precious trees – Which house our birds and feed our bees – Help save our trunks, branches and seeds – Take only the amount you REALLY need!"

In today's world, we are all being regularly reminded of our responsibility for caring for the environment, the need to recycle and saving on precious resources.

On the napkin, the emphasis was on the word 'really' –but my mind focussed on the word NEED (in comparison to what we may 'want.')

Put simply: a need is something you 'have to have' (to live and survive) – a want is something you 'would like to have.'

We will all have varying opinions as to what we see as a need compared to a want.

The Bible speaks often about the aspect of 'need' – and God promises time and time again through His word that 'He will meet all of our NEEDS.'

In addition to physical needs, we have emotional needs. When the psalmist was overcome by trouble and sorrow, he called on the name of the Lord.

He trusted in God to protect him and was able to declare, "... when I was in great need, He saved me." (Psalm 116:6)

God wants us to bring our needs to Him in our praying – even though He knows them before we ask. (See Matthew 6:8) By doing so, it acknowledges that we are trusting in His provision.

The writer of Hebrews encourages us to approach the throne of God's 'grace' with confidence, so that we may receive mercy and find grace to help us in our time of need. (Hebrews 4:16)

The apostle Paul knew what it was like to be in need – but at other times had plenty. He experienced times of being well fed but also times of going hungry. Fully relying on God 'for his own needs' – Paul was able to say to others, "My God will meet all your needs according to His glorious riches in Christ Jesus." (Philippians 4:19)

We will discover 'Jesus meets our every need' as we accept our need for Him – not just for what He does; but in trusting Him for who He is, as both Lord and Saviour of the world.

Come to God – and you will receive His mercy and find His grace

Crocuses in the compost

When I was taking some vegetable peelings to the compost heap in our garden, I noticed two crocus plants had taken root and flowered amidst the compressed vegetation. As I admired the fresh-looking purple petals – it reminded me how nice it is when we find something in 'unexpected places.'

Some of us may have had those 'retail moments' when we've found something we've been looking for, in a shop we deemed as unlikely to stock the item. I recall the time when I found a separate turntable for our Scrabble Game board – at a Hardware shop in a small town on Dartmoor!

Over the years as I've written 'Devotional thoughts' – my main purpose has been to reveal that God is able to make himself known in all things and in every situation. Those circumstances in our life – that may appear, mundane, routine or uninteresting to us – God is there – wanting to make His plan and purposes known.

At times; for many reasons, individuals or communities may feel neglected or forsaken. In my favourite Psalm in the Bible, God makes it clear; there is 'nowhere – where He is not present.'

David the psalmist asked, "Where can I go from your Spirit? Where can I flee from your presence?" He goes on to acknowledge, "If I climb to the sky, you're there! If I go underground, you're there! If I flew on morning's wings to the far western horizon, you'd find me in a minute – you're already there waiting!" (Psalm 139: 7-10 – The Message Bible)

The Bible is full of examples of people who found God in unexpected places, and as a result, experienced His blessings which are always evident when 'God is present.'

Joseph discovered God's plan and purpose for his life through his dreams. Moses heard God speak to him from within a burning bush. The Pharisees did not expect to find Jesus eating with sinners – but He was sharing with those whom He came to call to himself. Mary looked for Jesus in His tomb – but Jesus was standing behind her, 'alive' – calling her by name! Read the full exciting accounts in Genesis 37:5-11 / Exodus 3:1-4 / Matthew 9:9-13. /John 20:10-16 /

God desires to make himself known to each of us so we can know His love, forgiveness and grace towards us. After Job had suffered through all his testing trials, he said to the Lord, "My ears had heard of You but now my eyes have seen You." (Job 42:5)

If we are looking for God – He promises that we will find Him, even in the most unlikely and unforeseen situations.

Look around you today. God longs to speak to you and make himself known

Hearing or listening

We received a promotional flyer through our letter box saying, "Loves noisy restaurants, howling winds and back-seat drivers." As with many marketing slogans, I had to read further before I could understand what product it was referring to. The leaflet went on to outline the benefits of the 'most advanced hearing aid ever!'

One lady's testimony to her new hearing aid (who works as a National Coastwatch volunteer) said, "It's vital I can hear well – listening for distress calls from boats and radio transmissions ..."

As I read these words, it made me think about the importance of both hearing and listening. Hearing is a 'physical ability' (which hearing aids can help us with if required) but listening is a 'conscious choice' which will demand our attention and concentration. It is a learnt skill. To fully understand a person and acknowledge their true feelings – we need to listen to them with intention.

When I have the radio on in the back-ground when I'm working; I'm just hearing music – but when I take the time to sit down and play a CD through my headphones, I am actively listening to the music, words and individual sounds.

There are many references in the Bible which refer to the need to both hear from God and listen to Him.

God's word tells us, "... faith comes from hearing the message, and the message is heard through the word of Christ." (Romans 10:17)

One day when Jesus was teaching those who followed Him, He said, "Anyone with ears to hear should listen and understand." (Mark 4:9 – New Living Translation)

When we are truly listening to God's word; (not just hearing it) we will recognise the need to 'take action and put into practice' what Jesus commands, and place our faith in His promises, so they will become a reality in our lives. Jesus wants us to 'really listen' and 'consider carefully' every word He says to us.

Jesus' brother James wrote, "... be doers of the word, and not hearers only..." (James 1:22 – English Standard Version)

This week, as we read the scriptures we will hear from God. We demonstrate we have listened to Him as we do what He asks of us.

In addition, in the busyness of our days we may meet someone who needs to be listened to, and not just heard. As we take a few extra minutes to do that, it will make a world of difference to that person.

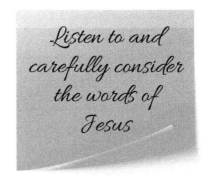

Listen to and
carefully consider
the words of
Jesus

Beautiful feet

I can remember when I was 12 years old visiting a Chiropodist on several occasions to have some verrucas treated on one of my feet. It was a quite long and painful experience getting rid of them. I went away on my first scout camp with a 'special sealant' on them to prevent infecting others.

A few years later I experienced the extreme itchiness from having 'athletes foot.' I recall one day at school – when the irritation was so severe – I took my shoe off outside and scratched the bottom of my foot along the ground to get relief. (Not a recommended treatment!)

As an adult – I've also had a corn causing pain, especially when walking down the many steps leading into town. I had a chiropodist visit at home to treat this foot problem, and I was amazed at how 'painless' it was as she used a scalpel to cut away the layers of thickened skin. To date, my feet are now sorted!

It's not surprising; many of us may find feet unattractive. They sweat and smell – nails need constant attention and they may have some unsightly bumps.

Having said that, the Bible talks about us having 'beautiful feet.' The prophet Isaiah announced, "How beautiful on the mountains are the feet of those who bring good news, who proclaim peace, who bring good tidings, who proclaim salvation ..." (Isaiah 52:7)

Tired, dirty and perspiring feet are seen as beautiful when they walk to share and example the good news of the gospel of Jesus Christ.

When the apostle Paul wrote to believers in Ephesus, he used the illustration of putting on all the pieces of a Roman soldier's armour – to describe how we can be strong in the Lord and in His mighty power.

When it came to footwear Paul said, "... and with your 'feet fitted with the readiness' that comes from the gospel of peace." (Ephesians 6:15)

The gospel of peace is the Good News that we can know 'peace with God' – forgiveness for our sins as we look to Jesus. Living in right-relationship with God enables us to be prepared and have a firm-footed stability as we are called to live out and share this gospel of peace.

As we put on our shoes or tend to our feet this week – remember that God's Word enables us to walk securely and safely as we do what He asks. David the Psalmist declared concerning the Lord, "My steps have held to your paths; my feet have not slipped... He makes my feet like the feet of a deer; He enables me to stand on the heights." (Psalm 17:5, 18:33)

How beautiful are the feet of those who bring Good News

Recycled metal

We had a leaflet delivered to us asking the question – "Where does the metal you recycle end up?" On the front of the flyer there were pictures of a tin, aerosol, drink can and foil dish. As I opened the leaflet – the pictures changed to reveal they could be used to make kettles, watches, phones or cameras when recycled. The possibilities are endless!

When I saw my old baked bean tin could be used to make an electrical appliance, it reminded me of the principle of how 'God wants to transform us' – making, moulding and reshaping us into people who can be used for His greater purposes.

God doesn't see and dwell on what we are like now – or were in the past – with all our faults and failings. When we come to Jesus and receive His forgiveness for our sins – God blots out our transgressions and remembers our sins no more. (Read Isaiah 43:25) He sees our potential for each new day, because 'He is the source of potential' in us.

God is the giver of all gifts, talents and abilities. As we seek to follow His ways – He will reveal our future potential which is found in our unused strengths, hidden talents and untapped capabilities. Someone once said, "Life is like a 15-speed bike. Most of us have gears we never use."

God gives the ability to use (to maximum potential) every gift He has given us, to serve Him and others.

Paul the apostle proclaimed, "I can do everything through Him (the Lord) who gives me strength." (Philippians 4:13)

Skills and talents take time to develop and practice. Potential has to be cultivated and continually worked on.

Potential is all about what we can do, but have not accomplished yet. 'God potential' can only come about with His help – and not striving alone in our strength and efforts.

The writer of Proverbs reminds us to, "Trust in the Lord with all your heart and lean not on your own understanding; in all your ways acknowledge Him, and He will make your paths straight." (Proverbs 3:5-6)

This week, as you recycle your old metal items – remember the seeds of potential God has planted within you – for using your time, resources and skills for His glory and the benefit of blessing others.

God is the source of our potential

Everlasting

When my jeans start to wear thin on the knees or the pockets get holes in – I store them under the wardrobe to keep them separate – and put them on when I'm either gardening or decorating.

Over the years we all see our upholstery and carpets fade and wear out. Nothing lasts or stays in good condition forever – things deteriorate, disintegrate, break down or seize up.

In contrast, the Bible reveals that God himself is Everlasting. The prophet Isaiah asks, "Do you not know? Have you not heard? The Lord is the everlasting God, the Creator of the ends of the earth. He will not grow tired or weary, and His understanding no-one can fathom." (Isaiah 40:28)

The Psalmist reminds us, "For the Lord is good and His love endures for ever; 'His faithfulness continues' through all generations." (Psalm 100:5)

If you want to be assured of the Lord's continuing love – read Psalm 136. Twenty-six times – you will read the phrase – "His love endures forever."

God reveals His enduring love through His goodness towards us – in making the heavens, spreading out the earth and in His great wonders. He is the God of gods and Lord of lords.

No one is exempt from pain, suffering and trials, but God promises to be a 'sure refuge' for always – to those who look to Him. When our mind and thoughts are stayed on God and His Word – He will keep us in perfect peace.

When we follow Jesus – a new path unfolds before us. The Bible says, "Your new life will last forever because it comes from the eternal, living word of God." (1 Peter 1:23 – New Living Translation) Jesus promised that 'His words will never pass away. They bring life, healing, hope and wholeness.

Over the years, we have all seen fads in clothing, gadgets and hairstyles – the list is long. When I was a teenager; I found it difficult to think that high waisted, baggie trousers would go out of fashion! Popularity in fads – can fade as quickly as it grows.

However, when it comes to God's plan and purpose for our lives – "the works that Jesus accomplishes through those who trust in Him are enduring, constantly maturing and have an eternal significance."

When Paul the apostle encountered difficulties in His mission for God, he was able to proclaim, "For our light and momentary troubles are achieving for us an 'eternal glory' that far outweighs them all." (2 Corinthians 4:17).

The LORD is the Everlasting God

God's workmanship

Some years ago, I recall on several occasions stopping underneath the Old Fish Market in Brixham, to observe the craftsmen working on a new mast for the Vigilance sailing trawler. The Vigilance was the last wooden trawler built at Uphams Yard, Brixham in 1926.

I was interested to read that the timber for the main mast came from the Kielder Forest in Northumberland. It was cut from a Douglas fir – which was over 80 years old. It measured just over 60 foot high and weighed two and a half tons. I pondered on the time it had taken for the tree to grow – and the dedication of the craftsmen as they shaped the wood into a working mast.

I was reminded of the words the apostle Paul spoke to the Church in Ephesus when he was explaining to them about the grace of Jesus Christ. He said "For we are God's workmanship, created in Christ Jesus to do good works"... (Ephesians 2:10)

God is able to shape and re-shape our lives – and enable us to do the works that He has prepared for us.

Jeremiah the prophet received instruction from the Lord to visit a potter's house; and there, God would reveal His message.

When Jeremiah arrived, he saw the potter working at his wheel – but the pot he was shaping from the clay was marred in his hands; so the potter formed it into another pot, shaping it as seemed best to him… "Like clay in the hand of the potter, so are you in my hand…" (Jeremiah 18:1-6)

Isaiah also reminds us that we need to allow God to shape and mould us. He said of the Lord – "We are the clay, you are the potter; we are all the work of your hand." (Isaiah 64:8)

As a treat for my birthday – I had the joy of taking a morning sail on board the Vigilance trawler. It was great to see the mast (that had once been just tree wood on the harbour side) now carrying the sail – which propelled the trawler through the water.

God is able to take the mundane things in our lives – our failures, mistakes, shattered dreams and our weaknesses, and as we invite Him to shape our lives – we can be transformed into a masterpiece for use in His plans and purposes.

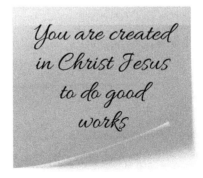

You are created
in Christ Jesus
to do good
works

Keep on keeping on

I was watching the 160th Oxford and Cambridge boat race on the TV. The 4.2-mile course of River Thames between Putney and Mortlake, provides the challenge for the two rowing teams to put to the test; all the hard training they have done during the year. Sadly, for Cambridge that year – their number 2 rower was briefly unseated following a clash of oars, and Oxford simply cruised away to victory by 11 lengths.

When this incident happened, the TV commentator explained how vital it would be for the Cambridge Cox to keep his team going as only he could see the distance that Oxford were ahead. With victory way out of sight – he needed great perseverance to encourage his crew just to complete the race.

After the race the unseated Cambridge rower commented, "I'm proud of the guys for the way they kept going, and I'll be up for the fight next year. You never want to lose like that, but you keep your head high and move on."

Perseverance is that quality that makes us persistent in doing something – despite difficulty or delay in achieving success.

When the apostle Paul wrote to the believers in Rome, he explained that they could rejoice; even in their suffering – because they knew that suffering produces perseverance, and perseverance produces character, which in turn leads to hope that does not disappoint. (Read Romans 5:3-5)

Jesus' brother James reminds us to "Consider it pure joy my brothers, whenever you face trials of many kinds, because you know that the testing of your faith develops perseverance. Perseverance must finish its work so that you may be mature and complete, not lacking anything. (James 1:2-4)

Job, In all his suffering and troubles; persevered – and God brought about an outcome that revealed His compassion and mercy. The Lord blessed the latter part of Job's life more than the first. (Read Job 42:12-17)

Don't give up or give in – to the tough challenge you may be facing today. Be encouraged by the blessing that Paul gave to the Church of the Thessalonians when they needed to stand firm and be strengthened. "May the Lord direct your hearts into God's love and Christ's perseverance." (2 Thessalonians 3:5)

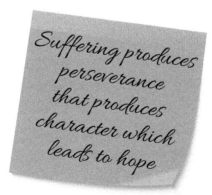

Suffering produces perseverance that produces character which leads to hope

Choosing seeds

I'm not an experienced gardener– but over the years it has been good to plant some vegetable seeds, in the hope that we would see some return.

With any home-grown veg – there is always a satisfaction as we serve those first of the season carrots and beans; and 'taste the reward' for the hard work of regular watering, weeding, and pest control – that is required when growing your own vegetables. The picture of the fully ripe crop on the front of the seed packet makes a good reminder that 'we hope to reap what we sow.'

In the Bible, we will discover that the principle of sowing and reaping is one that God calls us to practice. The apostle Paul wrote to the Church in Galatia saying – "A man reaps what he sows..." (Read Galatians 6:7-8)

Again; to the Church in Corinth, Paul reminds them that "Whoever sows sparingly will also reap sparingly, and whoever sows bountifully will also reap bountifully." (2 Corinthians 9:6)

Some of our vegetable crops over the years; have been better than others – but we continue to sow. In the same way, the Bible encourages us saying "let us not grow weary of doing good, for in due season 'we will reap, if we do not give up'. So then, as we have opportunity, let us do good to everyone ..." (Galatians 6:9-10)

This week; as we meet and talk with friends and neighbours – or even strangers – we will encounter those moments when we can sow positive things into their lives.

Moments: when we can choose to sow seeds of encouragement instead of criticism; seeds of forgiveness rather than bitterness, and seeds of love rather than envy and gossip.

As we sow these biblical attributes – God uses them to change and affect other people's lives for the good.

The writer of Proverbs said – "... he who refreshes others will himself be refreshed." (Proverbs 11:25)

God also desires that we use our time, money and other resources – to be a seed of blessing as we share them with others.

The Message Bible puts it this way." This most generous God who gives seed to the farmer that becomes bread for your meals is more than extravagant with you. He gives you something you can then give away, which grows into full-formed lives, robust in God, wealthy in every way, so that you can be generous in every way ..." (2 Corinthians 9:10-11)

If we sow bountifully we will reap bountifully

In the footsteps of Jesus

On the radio, I heard an advert for a holiday trip to the Holy Land, which invited people to 'come and walk where Jesus walked.'

I have never been abroad and the furthest north I've travelled in the UK is Leeds with the furthest south being The Lizard in Cornwall. However; I've got a passport – so I'm ready to go overseas if I choose to.

One person commented after taking their first trip to Israel, "My faith is rooted in events that occurred in real places."

Although I have not visited the Holy Land to walk where Jesus walked; I do have a handful of small stones that came from the Sea of Galilee, which remind me of the time when Jesus was walking there – and He called His first disciples saying "Come, follow Me." (Read Matthew 4:18-22)

Jesus continues to call each of us today. It's not a call to walk 'where' He walked – but a call to walk 'how' He walked. Whoever claims to live in God – must walk as Jesus walked. (1 John 2:6)

When Jesus was teaching about serving one another, He washed His disciple's feet. After finishing He said "Now that I, your Lord and Teacher, have washed your feet, you should also wash one another's feet. 'I have set you an example' that you should do as I have done for you." (John 13:14-15)

We may not live in a culture where we wash each other's feet – but there are many other ways in which we can serve, help and bless our family, friends and neighbours.

Paul the apostle also taught that 'our attitude should be the same as that of Christ Jesus.' (See Philippians 2:5-11)

He goes on to outline, we are to 'walk the way of selflessness and humility' just as Jesus did.

When we choose to follow Jesus, He will always give us His strength, ability and courage to enable us. He knows and understands what you are going through this week. You are not on your own! The writer of the book of Hebrews tells us – Jesus is able to sympathise with our weaknesses, and was tempted in every way, just as we are – yet was without sin.

Isaiah the prophet said of the Lord, "He will teach us His ways, so that we may walk in His paths ... Come let us walk in the light of the Lord." (Isaiah 2:3b, 5)

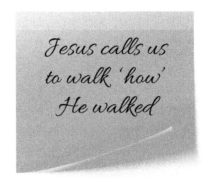

Jesus calls us to walk 'how' He walked

Lingering scent

When I get to the check-out at my local health and beauty drug-store, I am often asked if I would be interested in any of the latest fragrances which are on offer.

Looking at some advertisements, I read about how producers of perfumes select 'zesty notes of lemon, orange or mandarin and sophisticated florals' to call to mind fresh spring mornings and sunny days. In contrast; crisp sea-salt and even rich coffee – create scents that hint of warmth – even on the coldest winter day.

I recall walking past a young lady one day on my way home, but the fragrance she was wearing lingered in the air where she had been walking.

Perfume experts say a fragrance's worth-it-ness is judged on its staying power or 'sillage' (French for 'wake') and it's used to describe a scents trail, that stays in the air behind you as you walk down the street.

In the Bible, John records a time when a dinner was given in Jesus' honour. Mary took an expensive perfume and poured it on Jesus' feet and wiped His feet with her hair.

We are told the house was filled with the fragrance of the perfume. (John 12:1-3) In doing this, Mary was demonstrating her love and devotion to Jesus. Her worship was pleasing to the Lord.

Paul explained to the Church in Corinth, "For we are to God the aroma of Christ..." (2 Corinthians 2:15) and to the Church in Ephesus he said, "... live a life of love, just as Christ loved us and gave himself up for us as a 'fragrant offering' and sacrifice to God." (Ephesians 5:2)

Just as a little scent can fill a whole room – our small acts of kindness to people can make a big difference to them – leaving a lasting fragrance!

We can be the fragrance of Christ when we share scripture and speak true and encouraging words to those who may seek our guidance and advice. "The heartfelt counsel of a friend is as sweet as perfume and incense." (Proverbs 27:9 – New Living Translation)

As we follow Jesus, our lives should leave a fragrance for others to sense the character of God in us. When we are loving, patient, forgiving and kind towards others – we spread the fragrance of Christ. We are to be the 'scent' of God's kingdom, love and power as we live out our lives in obedience to His Word.

Acts of love and kindness leave a lasting fragrance

School desk

On commencing cleaning of a new zone at the College where I used to work, I observed a desk in one of the class rooms which in addition to being covered in 'doodles and interesting messages' – had a varnish-like coating on it which came off as you scrubbed it.

Over the next year (as I had time) I made a determined effort to restore this table – little by little, day by day – washing off newly posted comments and slowly taking the surface down to its original colour. By the end of the summer term, my project was completed. Mission accomplished!

This reminded me about what it is like to walk as a disciple of Jesus. As we seek Him and read God's Word, He reveals those areas in our life that need attention.

Discipleship is a life-long process of becoming more like Jesus in our attitudes, actions, thinking and motives.

Paul the apostle said, "... for it is God who works in you to will and to act according to His good purpose." (Philippians 2:13)

The things we 'practice' become our habits. The Bible reveals those 'good and beneficial habits' that we are to work on and establish in our lives.

Paul told the believers at Philippi to – "Do everything without complaining or arguing, so that you may become blameless and pure ..." (Philippians 2:14)

We will still fall short and fail along the way – but Jesus always lifts us to our feet again. He is patient, faithful, and forgiving towards us – as we 'press on' in becoming more like Him.

After Novak Djokovic won the Wimbledon Lawn Tennis Championship in 2015 – John McEnroe commented on Djokovic's game, saying …"it is pretty hard not to think he is getting stronger and stronger."

We will go from 'strength to strength' in our walk with God – as we commit to, and practice being doers of the word, and not hearers only. (See James 1:22)

Day by day – as we faithfully continue to live as followers of Jesus, we will discover "…the Lord – who is Spirit – makes us more and more like Him as we are changed into His glorious image." (2 Corinthians 3:18 – New Living Translation)

Discipleship is our daily commitment to becoming more like Jesus

The Well

Some years ago, we had our garage rebuilt. When we talked through our requirements with the builder, we agreed we would like the gutter to take rain-water from the flat roof – into a water butt. The water stored in the butt has been very useful for watering plants, washing drains, cleaning the car and also 'flushing the toilet!'

I've renamed the water butt – and I call it 'The Well.' At times (when I'm filling up my buckets) I'm reminded to pray for people in other countries who have to travel miles each day to collect their water for drinking and cooking, and it is more than likely – their water is not as clean as the water stored in our butt.

I read that by 2050, at least 1 in 4 people are likely to live in a country affected by chronic or recurring 'shortages of fresh water.' On the other end of the scale, floods account for 15% of all deaths related to natural disasters.

Water (known also as H_2O – 2 parts hydrogen, 1 part oxygen) is one of the most essential elements to health. It makes up more than two thirds of human body weight, and without water – we could die within days.

In the Bible, there are hundreds of references to this vital resource of water. In John's gospel, we read of a day when Jesus (tired from his journey) came and sat down by Jacob's well in a town called Sychar.

When a Samaritan woman came to draw water, Jesus asked her, "Will you give me a drink?" (Read the full story in John 4:4-26)

Jesus used the need for 'drinking water' to tell this woman about 'living water' that He alone can give. He explained, "Everyone who drinks this water (from the well) will be thirsty again, but whoever drinks the water I give him will never thirst. Indeed, the water I give him will become in him a spring of water welling up to eternal life." (John 4:13-14)

In our own strength and selfishness, we can pursue many things in life that do not bring lasting contentment or true satisfaction. However: as we 'thirst' (seek after) God's blessing, mercy, grace and friendship, Jesus promises we will be filled with His living water that satisfies – and never runs dry!

As we drink or use water as a resource this week, may it remind us that Jesus offers His living water through the Holy Spirit of God.

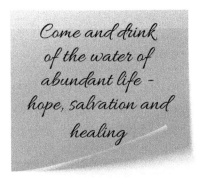

Come and drink of the water of abundant life – hope, salvation and healing

51

What is your first thought?'

Back in May 2018 – BBC Radio Devon listed a Top 10 List of 'first thoughts' people had on waking up. They included: the weather, tasks to do, work, health, what's on social media? What day of the week is it? What shall I wear? Do I need to wash my hair? Morning commute and family troubles.

It is important to fix our thoughts on something good and positive on waking. David the psalmist started his day in prayer. In Psalm 4:3 he says – "Morning by morning, O LORD you hear my voice; morning by morning I lay my requests before You and wait in expectation."

We could also acknowledge and declare, "This is the day the LORD has made, I will rejoice and be glad in it." (See Psalm 118:24)

In these times and days in which we live – it is vital that we keep our thoughts focussed on God and His salvation, love, peace, hope and encouragement that He bestows upon us.

David the psalmist reminds us that the LORD perceives our thoughts from afar. He knows now, what you are thinking. Before that thought is expressed via your tongue, He knows it completely. (Psalm 139:2, 4)

Paul the apostle gives sound advice for how we are to either train or control our thinking. "We are to take every thought captive to Jesus to make it obedient to Him." (2 Cor 10:5)

As we share any anxious thoughts with the Lord and cast our cares on Him, because He cares for us – we can leave the outcome to God.

Again, when Paul wrote to the believers in Philippi, he instructed them to 'choose' what to think about. When fears and irrational thoughts come our way, we must take intentional action and start to think about things which are true, noble, right, pure, lovely, admirable, excellent or worthy of praise. (Phil 4:6, 8, 9b) When we do this, the God of peace will be with us.

God is good all the time – His love endures forever. Think about His goodness – 'Now'

Christmas gifts

As Christmas Day draws near – most of us will have purchased and wrapped the presents that we are going to give to our family and friends. I came across a web-site that was giving advice on how to choose the best gift to give to someone.

The article informed me that when selecting a gift for a person; it needs to be something that is meaningful, of value to the receiver and personal.

The value of the gift isn't connected with the cost, but to the usefulness of the gift after Christmas is over. We can make a gift personal by adding an engraved or written message on it – which reminds the person each time they see it, that they are being thought of.

On the first Christmas; God knew exactly what gift the world needed. The people who were walking in darkness and sinfulness were in need of a Saviour – so God sent Jesus to save us from our sins. (Matthew 1:21)

"God didn't go to all the trouble of sending his Son merely to point an accusing finger, telling the world how bad it was. He came to help, to put the world right again." (John 3:17 – The Message Bible)

The Bible says – "The Father has sent His Son to be the Saviour of the world." (1 John 4:14) When Zechariah prophesied about Christ's birth, he proclaimed "Praise be to the Lord, the God of Israel, because He has come and redeemed His people." (Luke 1:68)

The angels announced they were bringing "Good news of great joy that will be for all people." Jesus came to bring his love, joy and peace to our world – "not just at Christmas time, but for every day of our lives". He will never leave or forsake those who put their trust in Him

God's gift to you is personal. He knows you by name; and by sending His Son from heaven to earth, He made the way open for "you" to know and experience His saving love and mercy.

As we give and receive gifts this Christmas – may we be thankful to God "for His Gift, precious, beyond telling, His indescribable, inexpressible, free Gift!" – of Jesus Christ. (2 Corinthians 9:15 Amplified Bible)